# Whippet Dogs as Pets

A Pet Guide for Whippet Dogs

Whippet Dogs General Info, Purchasing, Care, Cost, Keeping, Health, Supplies, Food, Breeding and More Included!

By Lolly Brown

# Foreword

Whippets are one of the unknown yet gentle and active breeds of dog. They are fitted for any kind of person who likes play, run around, but still slouch and sleep for hours.

These active cute dogs will literally run past you! They can run as fast as 35 mph, so you better catch them fast! It is worth noting that these fur buddies are easy to deal with people and noises at every age - they love company, even with strangers! They make great dog buddies but are not as great with little pets as they have a high prey drive. This breed is one of the unknown breeds but you will be sure that you will certainly like them!

Read this book and know more about this breed. Here, we will give you a detailed outline on pet basics, showing, feeding and nutrition guide, and so much more. Have fun reading and exploring the world of whippets!

# Table of Contents

# Introduction

Whippets were previously known as hunters of small game and rabbits, as well as the poacher's best friend. They are primarily known for their fly ball, rally, obedience, lure coursing, and great agility!

This creature is also known for its stylish look, friendly personality, as well as its unique nature. They make a great house companion as well as an amazing show dog. Aside from this, they can still hunt games if they are trained to do so. When you first see a Whippet, you will be sure that it is the perfect dog for you! They are friendly around strangers and guests, still can sleep long hours, has a medium size, and will not bark too much.

Simply say, a Whippet may alert you if there's danger, but will not really be true guard dog. A word of caution though, whippets tend to be in packs rather than to be alone. They are easy to be attached to their humans and other kids. They do not like to walk or run in the rain or snow, but very easy to house train.

With the advantages, there are also disadvantages about the Whippets. They have graceful yet muscular built. This build makes them excellent runners and jumpers. If something catches their attention, they will surely run after it, no matter how much you have trained it. Remember, your whippet can't roam around free and be kept around a leash all the time. If you plan on keeping it in an enclosure, make sure the fence is at least five feet tall.

You might think that taking care of a Whippet is an easy task. This is a different breed than your usual dogs. You need to have a lot of patience and attention to fully train this dog. Here, we will help you in making a decision whether a Whippet is a right fit for you. We will give you detailed information about them. Happy reading!

# Chapter One: History and Basic Characteristics

Whippets are one of the most common hunting dog, but not really a known house pet. Although it is bred to hunt through its eyes which give them the ability to focus on its prey, they can also love to their humans. They are both enthusiastic and athletic while playing or exercising but also tranquil and docile when at home, especially when surrounded by humans, children, and even guests.

Aside from those characteristics, Whippets are also gentle, quiet, intelligent, friendly, and lively which makes them an excellent pet choice - especially when you are living alone!

Whippets are also known as one of the most obedient breeds that easily adapts to moving to different homes. They are best suited for people who love to play and walk regularly; whippets will repay this with unconditional love and faithfulness. They, further, enjoy slouching at the foot of their master's feet as well as being with lively children.

Whippets are not high maintenance dogs. But, they are part of the athletic breed and needs to be exercised daily combining walking and running. They are natural sprinters and tend to run freely when they have freedom and big space. They can't stand cold weather as they have short hair and less body fats. Although they have short coat, they still need regular grooming.

In this book, we will give you other essential information, such as history and evolution of this dog breed. These information will guard and guide you in taking care and learning about this breed. We will help you in taking care of your Whippet, from the moment you purchase it until it gets sick.

## The Life History

Just like any other dog breed, Whippets have a colorful history. There are arguments saying that this breed has been around for about 150 to 200 years!

According to Mr. Frederick Freeman Lloyd, the Whippet was a mixture of the Greyhound and Terrier and was bred for racing purposes. Further, the Greyhound gives the Whippet the beautiful conformation, speed and stamina, while the Terrier blood gives it the tenacity and gameness. A beautiful mix, right?

The development began in the mid to late 1800s, when the Greyhound's abilities were needed. Working class families need Greyhound-like dogs but can't afford to keep one, so they created a mix breed that resulted to a smaller, less demanding Whippets. However, there are also talks that Whippets existed even before 1907! F.C. Hignett stated that Whippets existed even before pedigrees were official; however the Greyhound shares the same genealogy with Whippets.

Whippets are the most popular in the English sight hound family. They are bred as true racers although they are not as popular as Greyhound in this field.

Whippets have developed a keen eye, amazing sense of smell, flexible body that could easily track targets, run towards it, catch and deliver it to their humans.

Whippets quickly proved themselves as great hunters of small games and rabbits, it grew in popularity and refined throughout the years, it was recognized by the American Kennel Club (AKC) in 1888 while in 1891 in The Kennel Club of England.

## Notable Characteristics

Aside from the characteristics given above, our beloved Whippets have other notable characteristics you need to watch out for.

### Apartment Lovin'

Whippets generally have low energy levels while inside the house, but need exercise as they tend to be destructive and overactive if they will not be exercised.

### Loves Socialization

Your whippet is an undemanding and polite dog that would go great with family members, children, strangers, and different dogs. However, if you fail to socialize them properly, they will become stressed and timid.

You should train your Whippet in proper socialization especially if you have other pets staying with it. There were instances that whippets chased other little pets and sometimes injure it if not properly trained or socialized.

## Not a Watchdog

Although they are big dogs, they rarely bark and are very friendly towards anyone they will meet.

## Loves Exercise

As stated before, your Whippet will need a lot of exercise time and will enjoy running and romping around your fenced yard. But, remember to always keep your Whippet on leash as they will run fast and away from their owners as possible. If they will not be exercised, they will become very destructive. If they will be exercised, they will become calm and quiet.

## Strong Prey Drive

Whippets were primarily bred for hunting. This trait has been passed through to the current breed. Whippets will pursue their prey especially when they keep their focus on it.

## Very Easy to Groom

Aside from having short coat, your Whippet will not shed excessively. You only need to brush its coat once a week to remove loose hair.

**Great House Companion**

Whippets love companion especially children. However, you still need to teach your child to properly interact with dogs and you never leave your child with a dog alone.

## Quick Facts

**Origin:** England

**Pedigree**: crossbreed of Greyhound and many possible terriers

**Breed Size:** big size

**Body Type and Appearance:** Has a classic 'inverted s' line. It has a deep chest and trim waist. It has a lean head connected to a long, arched neck. They possess sturdy and slim legs that are combined with agile, fleet-footed athlete.

**Group:** Hound Group

**Height:** 19 - 22 in (Male), 18 - 21 in (Female)

**Weight:** 18 - 48 pounds. Males average 34 pounds and 29 pounds for female

**Coat Length:** short, close

**Coat Texture:** smooth and firm

**Color**: brindle, white, black, fawn, blue, red

**Temperament**: curious, playful, willing to approach people, affectionate, lively, gentle, intelligent, quiet, friendly

**Strangers**: friendly around strangers

**Other Dogs**: gets along well with other dogs

**Other Pets**: may get along well with other pets if properly socialized, may chase small pets

**Training**: loves to be trained by their humans

**Exercise Needs**: needs daily exercise through running or walking around a fenced yard

**Health Conditions**: generally healthy but may be affected by the following illnesses: aesthesia sensitivity, deafness, eye diseases, von willebrand's disease

**Lifespan**: average 12 to 15 years

We have just given you the basic information about our beloved Whippets. This information will help you in your everyday life with the dog. There is still a lot of information that you need to know in order to have a healthy and happy whippet. Read on to know more.

# Chapter Two: Owning Whippets

We have finished talking about the rich history and basic background of Whippets but, we will not stop there because there are a lot of things that you need to know! Whippets are wonderful household companions who need a lot of exercise. There are still other temperaments that you need to know about our dearest Whippets.

In this chapter, we will give you reasons why you should own a Whippet. We will be discussing how Whippets deal with other animals, temperament, compatibility with other dogs and animals, and how to purchase your own Whippet legally.

*What Makes It a Great Pet?*

Purchasing your first pet is a big decision, you must know every little detail about the pet you want to have: how it behaves, its characteristics, and care that it needs. Whippets are lovable creatures that do well with children, guests, and even strangers.

Whippets are loving, affectionate, and loyal dogs especially to their humans who walk and run with them. Although they are big dogs, they do well to small spaces because they like to slouch and snooze so much. They are easily adaptable, especially to new surroundings.

All in all, Whippets are great creatures for you to keep as pets. You can have a loyal dog that will wait and wag it's until for you.

## Temperament and Behavioral Characteristics

- They love to run.
- They need regular access to a large fenced area.
- They love to chase other animals that run around.
- Whippets think independently and will not care about pleasing you.
- They are gentle and quiet around the house.
- Whippets, however, still have a very strong prey instinct.

- Whippets will grow up to very quiet and dignified.
- Young whippets may be out of control.
- Whippets love to have company.
- They are generally friendly around other dogs.
- They love to play catch with other whippets and sighthounds.
- Male whippets are competitive.
- Whippet is very similar to Greyhound.
- They have two main personalities: a runner and a heavy sleeper.
- They have pretty sensitive feelings.
- They can tolerate hot weather but not cold weather.

## Behavioral Characteristics with other Pets

Whippets are great with other Whippets or same sized dogs. They can easily adapt to new environments and playmates easily. However, you must take caution into introducing little pets to your Whippet as they might get hurt or killed easily.

## Is Whippet Breed Right For You?

In this portion, we will be giving you pros and cons about Whippets. This will help you decide if you still want to pursue into buying your own Whippet:

## Pros

- A medium-sized Greyhound
- Looks great! It is elegant, slender, racy built, with a graceful and light - footed gait.
- They have sleek easy care coat.
- They are quiet and dignified, unobtrusive and undemanding when indoors.
- They like to run around, gallop, and play with breath taking speeds when outdoors.
- Whippets are generally polite to everyone.

## Cons

- They need a safe enclosed area where he can run around and play
- They need to chase other things that run around.
- If they are not properly socialized, they can get timid and fearful.
- Whippets are very independent; they will not please their owners.

- They are emotionally sensitive especially to abrupt changes in schedule and stress.

## Legal Requirements and Dog Licensing

If you really aim to own your own Whippet as your own pet, you should follow rules and regulations when owning one. Licensing requirements differ from states, regions, and countries.  In the United States, there are no strict requirements for owning dogs. However, some states might require you to acquire a license for your pet. Moreover, it is always the best option for you to obtain a license for your pet. A license will not only protect you but also your pup.

In this section, we will give you some guidelines on how to acquire licenses both in the United States and United Kingdom.

## United States Licensing for Dogs

There is no strict policy in licensing dogs. However, some states require dog owner to license and register their dogs.

**Steps in Licensing Your Pet**

**Step #1:** Provide enough proof that your Whippet has been vaccinated against rabies.

**Step #2:** Have your license renewed as well as your dog's vaccination records.

You only need $25 a year to purchase your dog's license. However, they might be additional things you need to provide in other states. Your license is only temporary until all the documents have been submitted.

If your region does not really require you to have your dog licensed, it is still the best path for you to go. If, unfortunately, your dog gets lost, an identification card will help you find him easily. Other than that, you can add an ID tag to its collar for additional identification.

## United Kingdom Licensing for Dogs

Contrary to the United States, the United Kingdom urges all the dog owners to license their pets when they have acquired it. However, dog owners from UK do not need to have their dogs vaccinated against rabies. The reason for this move is that UK has eradicated rabies completely.

Dog licenses need to be renewed annually and as cheap as in the United States. Moreover, you may need to obtain a special permit if you plan to travel out of the country with your pet.

## How Much Do I Need?

In this portion, we will give you a glimpse on the budget on how much you might need to take care and purchase your own Whippet. We will give you a rough estimate on how much you need for toys, licensing, grooming supplies, accessories, and etc.

## Are You Ready?

Having a dog is surely a big responsibility. You need to allot not only time, but also money, mind, and soul to this process. Having a new pet would mean additional budget for toys, grooming, treats, and food. You need to allot more money so your dog could live a happy and abundant life.

You need to create a budget plan to plot all the expenses you might have in the future. It starts with purchasing the dog, buying treats and foods, health care, and even accessories. It might be difficult to manage at first, but you will get a hang of it soon.

The total cost for all your expenses will heavily depend upon the availability and location of the resources needed. Also, some stores might raise their prices because they have low supply. Other than that, you need to take into consideration the quality and brand of the resources you will be buying. This part will help you know the breakdown of the budget you will need to raise your own Whippet.

## Price of a Whippet

There are a lot of things to consider before buying your pet Whippet. First you need to determine the cost.

Prices for puppies vary from region, Mid-Atlantic, New England, and the West Coast. Among the three, New England gives the most expensive price for the Whippet.

Whippets are mid-ranged dogs unlike purebred dogs. The prices start at $600 and can shoot up to $1500. You might be shocked by the prices, but knowing the popular of this breed.

## Other Essentials

There are other expenses that you will encounter when raising your own Whippet, these are vet consultation, bed, vaccinations, toys, food, treats, and others.

You might not feel that these things are not essential at first, but the aforementioned things are needed to raise your Whippet happy and healthy. It also makes their life more comfortable.

*Bed ($50 - $100)*

You might think that owning a bed is only a luxury rather than a necessity. However, there are reasons why you need to buy your pet a bed for its own:

✓ Your dog will feel secure.

✓ Your dog will feel that it has a 'special' place on its own.

✓ Dog's bed provide comfort for your pet. You wouldn't want your pet to be sleeping on the ground, dirt, or wood.

There are a lot to consider in buying your dog's bed, which are:

✓ Sleeping Style. Some dogs like to sleep all curled up, sprawled or being burrowed under the sheets.

✓ Dog's Size. Since our dearest Whippet is on the middle

to large size, you need to provide a big dog bed immediately. A big dog bed will enable your dog to be comfortable until it becomes an adult dog.

✓ Decor and budget. People have designed different dog beds for different function. Make sure you find one that best complements your home and style.

*Toys ($20-$50)*

Whippets love to play especially around their large fenced area. You may opt to buy few toys so your dog could have its own leisure time. However, you must designate the correct 'play' time at home. Remember, your Whippet may have vicious tendencies at home if left untrained.

*Grooming Tools ($50-$100)*

The Whippet only have silky coat which is pleasurable to touch and easy to maintain. This short coat will keep your house free from loose hair. Although it is not much of a necessity, you still need to groom him once in a while. You just need a weekly brushing to get rid of impurities and dead hair.

*Dog Food and Treats ($50-100)*

Food is a key to keeping your dog healthy and happy. Dog food has special added nutrients that will help your dog get enough vitamins and minerals it needs to have. Other than that, dog treats are used for obedience training as well as a yummy treat after a stressful day. However, you just don't buy the first dog food that you see; you need to research the nutritional value and its benefits to your dog's health.

## Medical Expenses

Medical expenses are inevitable for anyone. There will be many expenses that your dog will encounter, such as spay/neuter surgery, vaccination, micro-chipping, and vet consultation. You might think that these are only seasonal expenses, but you need to save up in case you need to have these surgeries.

## Micro-chipping

Micro-chipping is a task that will help keep your dog safe; a chip will be implanted under your dog's skin. The chip carries a lot of information about its owner. The price of the procedure is only $50, but might vary in some states.

Micro-chipping is a not a requirement in both the United States and United Kingdom, but it will keep your dog safe from any harm.

## Initial Vaccinations

Vaccinations are needed if you have purchased your Whippet at an early stage. Initial vaccines and boosters can easily defend the puppies against common viral infection, if they are given at the correct age.

Mothers will give essential antibodies that will defend the puppies at an early age; however, vaccines provide additional care against viruses and diseases. The price of the vaccine starts at $50.

## Spay/Neuter Surgery

One of the hardest decisions that you will make is whether you will spay/neuter your pet. If you don't want to breed or take care of more puppies, it is best for you to go to this path. There are several benefits of spay/neutering your pet, they are:

✓ Lessen the chances of uterine infection, testicular cancer, breast cancer

✓ Eliminate unwanted litter from the bunch

✓ Your pet won't go into heat and find a mate.

There are two factors affecting the price of the surgery: the gender and the location of the clinic.

## Veterinary Consultations

Another must for your pet is veterinary consultations. You must keep yourself and your vet updated on the health of your Whippet to continually keep it healthy. Whippets need regular check - ups to keep it vaccinated and to see whether they are healthy or not. The cost of veterinary visit starts from $40 and above. Keep a rainy day fund for medicine and consultation.

# Chapter Three: Purchasing a Whippet Dog

In this portion, we will talk about where to buy your Whippet and how to spot a great reputable breeder. Also, we will have some tips and techniques to help you figure out what kind of Whippet you need. There are many things for you to consider in finding the best possible place for you buy your Whippet.  A healthy breed will create a happy pet in the future. There are tell-tale signs for you to know if the breeder is untrustworthy or not.

## *What Kind of Whippet Do I Want?*

You have now decided to buy a Whippet, now there comes an even bigger decision: What kind of whippet do I want? You may want a higher-needs puppy or even an adult, but, you need to assure that your Whippet is in the right hands and you can commit into taking care of it fully.

### Buying a Puppy

Most people opt for this choice because of they want to raise the pet on their own from the start. If you can commit fully and like to run around and train your puppy Whippet, you can choose this option. However, you should be reminded that a puppy whippet requires more work as they get very playful especially with cats.

### Buying an Adult

Buying an adult dog is another choice for you. Adult Whippets which are housebroken, crate-trained, socialized, and leased trained are the popular choice for people who have no time to fully take care and train their Whippets.

Many owners would take care of puppy whippets until the age of 2, but then decide that the pet is not for them, of if the Whippet is not turning to be a show quality dog, but rather a house companion.

Many owners prefer this choice because these kinds of dogs are already housebroken, and they might not be easily available again. However, some of these dogs are rehomed due to behavioural problems. You need to connect with the breeder to know the real characteristics of the dog that you will be purchasing. Some breeders might even get back the dog that they have sold especially if they have seen that their dog has some sort of problems. Adult whippets easily trust their new owners, especially those who care, love, and give food for them.

## Rescued Dog

The WRAP (Whippet Rescue and Placement) is the US national rescue organization especially for Whippets. They are an independent rescue group, but most volunteers are also from the American Whippet Club. Aside from WRAP, there are other organizations and people who rescue and foster dogs until they have new homes.

Adult Whippets who lost their home but not their fault, sometimes due to their family emergencies, job transfers, old owners, and etc. are some of the adult whippets who are in foster care. There are counsellors who will talk to you about adopting your own adult whippet and what kind of shelter it needs. You need to have an open heart and mind to take care of an adult whippet that has lost its home. However, whippets will repay you with utmost love and affection it can give. You just need to pay small adoption fee but is just a small cost than a puppy.

## Race-bred, Show-bred, Lure Coursing-bred, or a combination?

There are many reasons why a breeder would want to breed a Whippet; some might breed it for show, race, lure, or even a combination of all of these. You need to find a dog that will fit your dog's personality, as you will spend a lot of time with it. A good breeder would even tell you the characteristics of the dog that would fit for your own personality.

### *The Responsible Whippet Breeder*

Responsible breeders both produce puppies for competitiveness and companionship. You can know if the breeder is serious if s/he is breeding for talent, speed, or quality. You may need to be a part of a Whippet community to know how to spot a great breed. Other than that, great breeders always test their pet's health. They test the parents for any diseases that may affect the eyes or even its heart.

You may want to visit the breeder to see if the Whippet is in good health and great weight, housed properly, outgoing, socialized, and friendly.

You can see how the breeder has trained his/her litters through its reaction with other puppies. Although they are many, cages should not have foul odors or even dirty. You may also want to meet the parents to get to know the background and history of the dog that you will buy.

In turn, your breeder will need to ask lot of questions from you, to know if you will be a responsible dog owner in the future and if their puppy will get a happy home. You should answer the questions honestly and don't be offended with the questions s/he might ask. The questions asked by the breeder will be the test of your loyalty and personality for the pet. In this portion, you can also ask the breeder essential questions and in turn, they might give recommendations such as training, housing, and feeding your own puppy. You might also be asked of the area around your house in which the puppy may need to run to.

*Twelve Points You Need To Remember In Finding a Great Breeder*

There are points for you to consider into finding a great breeder to purchase your puppy from. It is your responsibility to find and search for the best breeder in your town. You may need to find the breed standard, color, size, traits, and etc. about the breed to fully understand what you are looking for.

Here are the guidelines for you to consider into finding a quality breeder, if your breeder doesn't pass these qualifications, find another one:

- Provides you with a checklist about the adult dogs or the puppies before selling them. They will give you the health problems faced by the dogs and the checks done to fix the problems.

- Have a lifetime 'return' policy. Great breeders will do everything they can to help their Whippets find a great home. If you can't provide for care anymore, your breeder may help you find another home for your Whippet.

- Great breeders may want an application form from you. Whippets are mainly bred for companionship and competitiveness. Breeders have spent a lot of time for their dogs just to give it to anyone. They want their puppies to have a healthy and happy home.

- A responsible breeder will let you know everything about your Whippet. S/he will let you know all the needs and temperaments of your furry friend. Different breeds have their own set of characteristics. A great breeder will let you know if the Whippet is already housebroken or not, or if the Whippet has a high prey drive, or if it does not like small children, or if it is just an indoor dog.

- There will be a specific contract with a set of requirements and guarantees. You will need to sign the contract because it involves a lot of information about your Whippet. However, you should not make a deal with a breeder who promises great things for such a short period of time.

- The breeder should a health record of the puppy. S/he must have all the dates involving the whelping, problems, dates of worming, vaccinations, and etc. This information will be essential to your vet and to you. However, if these things are just a given orally or written on a scrap paper, the breeder is not really reputable. Walk away and find a new breeder.

- The breeder will open their house to you. You will have an opportunity to meet the parents, place where s/he keeps the puppies. You can inspect if the atmosphere is clean, friendly, warm, and healthy. You should not make a deal with a breeder who will only invite you to a parking lot.

- A great breeder will only breed on or two dog breeds. A great breeder will specialize in only one or two breeds. S/he must have spent time getting to know the breed, heritage, requirements, needs, health, and temperament.

- A learned breeder will know how to socialize the puppies. If you see the puppies, you will know that they are acquainted with one another and its home environment. See warning signs of not taking care of the dog properly, such as isolation. An isolated puppy will not socialize properly with anyone or any animal.

- An actual breeder will advise you to take home a puppy if it is only at least eight weeks old. You should confirm its age with the records kept by the breeder. A learned breeder knows the ins and outs of the mom and its litter. If a breeder will allow you to take home the dog easily, turn back because they are just in it for the cash, not for proper breeding.

- Lastly, an amazing breeder will always be free to answer any of your questions. S/he will give you all the contact information and is open to any questions you may have. They will also give you their address and invite you to visit their place. If the breeder is difficult to find, or does not want to give additional information about him/herself, you should not buy from him/her.

## Characteristics of a Healthy Breed

Whether you are planning to buy a baby or adult wood turtle, you need to keep in mind several characteristics in having the best breed possible.

First, you need to look at its eyes. Make sure that the eyes are free from any discharge or any other cloudiness. Also, you need to look at its breathing, make sure that there is no difficulty in breathing and no discharge from the nose. You should ask the breeder for any other specific information that you might want to know. Also, the wood turtle must be mobile and can move at its will.

Never acquire a wood turtle if it has suspicious markings or signs of health issues. Inspect the shell and body and make sure there is no parasite infection.

## List of Breeders and Rescue Websites

We have provided you with different kinds of Whippets to buy. In this part, we encourage you to try and foster an adult Whippet.

Aside from that, these sites will give you all the information you need about your pet. These groups are knowledgeable about any topic regarding your pet Whippet. Here is the list of breeders and adoption rescue websites around United States and United Kingdom:

### United States Breeders and Rescue Websites

### Adopt a Pet

<https://www.adoptapet.com/s/adopt-a-whippet>

### Whippet Rescue and Placement (WRAP)

<http://whippet-rescue.org/>

### Northern California Whippet Fanciers Association

<http://www.ncwfa.com/whippet-rescue.html>

## All Breed Rescue

<http://www.allbreed-rescue.org/special_breeds/adopted/adopted.html>

## Timberblue Whippets

<http://www.timbreblue.com/rescue/whippet-rescue>

## TheWhippet.net

<https://www.thewhippet.net/whippet-rescue.html>

## Greyhound Rescue Austin

<http://www.greyhoundrescueaustin.com/adoption.php>

## A Place For US Greyhounds

<https://www.aplaceforusgreyhounds.org/>

## Niagra Dog Rescue

<http://www.niagaradogrescue.org/>


**Utah Whippet**

<http://www.utahwhippet.com/pages/rescue.html>


**United Kingdom Breeders and Rescue Websites**

**Just Whippets Rescue**

<https://www.justwhippetsrescue.co.uk/>


**JR Whippet Rescue**

<https://whippetrescue.org.uk/>


**Greyhound and Lurcher Rescue**

<https://www.greyhoundandlurcherrescue.co.uk/dogs.aspx>


**Hounds First Sighthound Rescue**

<http://houndsfirst.co.uk/>


**Bring Joy, Adopt a Dog**

<http://www.dogsblog.com/category/whippet/>

## The Kennel Club

<https://www.thekennelclub.org.uk/services/public/findares cue/display.aspx?id=2625>

## Southern Lurcher Rescue

<http://www.southernlurcherrescue.org.uk/needinghomes.p hp>

## Evesham Greyhound and Lurcher Rescue

<http://www.lurcher.org.uk/>

## Greyhound Rescue NorthEast

<http://www.greyhoundrescuenortheast.com/>

## Whippet Rescue UK

<https://www.pets4homes.co.uk/classifieds/1096357- whippet-rescue-uk-prince-sandbach.html>

## Norfolk Greyhound Rescue

<http://norfolkgreyhoundrescue.co.uk/>

## Lozzas Lurcher Rescue

<http://www.lozzaslurcherrescue.co.uk/>

## Kent Greyhound Rescue

<http://www.kentgreyhoundrescue.com/>

## Allsorts Dog Rescue

<http://www.allsortsdogrescue.org.uk/>

## Blue Cross for Pets

<https://www.bluecross.org.uk/rehome/dog>

## Many Tears Animal Rescue

<http://www.manytearsrescue.org/>

## Grinshill Animal Rescue

<https://www.grinshillanimalrescue.co.uk/>

**Northern Greyhound Rescue**

<http://www.northerngreyhoundrescue.org.uk/>

**Bedlington Terrier Rescue**

<http://www.bedlingtonrescue.co.uk/>

Here, we have listed websites that will help you gain more knowledge about Whippets. Make sure you allot time to go through each site to gain additional information about your desired pet. You now have an idea what kind of pet you want to have in the future, it is now up to you to decide what kind of Whippet you will take home. Let's now continue the journey in knowing our beloved pet.

# Chapter Four: A Sustainable Home for Our Furry Friend

Whippets are amazing pet companions; they are easily adaptable to changes and new environment. They can get accustomed to new traditions easily. Having a Whippet is not easy. You need to master everything that you can about the breed, such as housing requirements, vet requirements, amount of exercise, feeding, and etc. Taking care of a Whippet is just like taking care of your own child, you take care of it from the very first days of its life, until its last breath. In this portion, we will give you tips on how to give a healthy and happy life for your Whippet. We have also included puppy proofing to avoid any accidents in the near future.

*Housing Requirements*

Whippets are big dogs, and you need to be constantly reminded of that. Although they are big, they can live in small spaces as long as they have a big fenced area to run around. They want long walks that will eat up their energy to lose the excess weight. Here are the housing requirements for your dog::

- Bed or Crate
- Collar, leash, and harness
- Food and water dishes
- Toys
- Grooming supplies
- Blanket

These are just some of the housing requirements that you need to give to your pet, you might think they are excessive, but they will help in making your dog's life wonderful and peaceful.

**Bed or Crate**

We need to give a big bed for your Whippet, so it can enjoy the space and will not be constraint about movement. You can also throw in pillows and bed sheets for just an extra touch.

Some owners see that new puppies feel safe and comfortable when they have their own space for them. This makes them easier to adjust to a new environment. You may want to buy Whippet its own cage, but it is totally your own decision in buying a cage. A cage may help you transport your dog easily, but it can cause temperament shift easily.

## Collar, Leash and Harness

Collars, leashes, and harnesses are important things for your Whippets. Collars add certain security for your dog's tags and licenses. Make sure that the collar will fit correctly, not too tight, not too loose. You also need to buy a leash for your dog. The leash is important especially when walking, running, or even playing with the dog. It prevents any accidents to happen. Harness will enable you to control all of your dog's movement when you are walking, playing, or running. Other than that, it lessens the pressure on your dog's neck. These things are important to promote happiness and comfort during walks and plays for your dog.

## Toys

Although Whippets are very playful and active creatures, you should not give them too much toys to play with.

Toys can trigger certain temperaments that might be harmful to kids or other small pets. You need to contain their activity when outside or when just playing. You need to teach your dog when to play or when to just slouch.

## Grooming Supplies

Luckily for you, Whippets only have short coat. Later on in this book, you can find more information on how to properly groom your pet.

## Food/Water Dishes

Food and Water bowls are important to your pets. It varies in sizes and shapes but you need one that will suit your dog best. Whippets are big creatures; they need a big bowl because they need to be fed a lot, on a small interval. You need to possess a ceramic bowl and stainless steel that won't have many bacteria build - up in the future. You need to have these things in a sturdy form as you will use them for very long amount of time.

*Housing Temperature*

Housing temperature is a key factor in keeping your dog happy. You need to provide an adequate temperature for your dog. It can stand medium to hot temperature, but not really cold temperature due to its short coat. You can have your heater up and constantly check up your Whippet. You do not want a sick Whippet in your home due to coldness.

*Guidelines on How to Keep Your Pup Happy and Safe*

Puppy - proofing your home is just like creating child-proof environment. There are things that you need to do to have a happy life with your Whippet:

✓ **Keep your trashes away.** A curious puppy will sniff and eat your trash. It is best to keep your trashes neatly stored or in a place where it is inaccessible by your pet. You do not what kind of food your dog might eat when it is rummaging your trash can.

✓ **No visible cords.** You don't want your new puppy to be accidentally shocked, burned, or even causing small fires. You need to supervise your dog not to get curious too much or it may cause serious injuries.

✓ **Keep your bags away.** Avoid accidental Xylitol poisoning if you keep your bags away. Many bags, such as gym bag, diaper bag, purse, or even a backpack contains this.

✓ **Keep your (medicated) drugs away).** Human medicine is one of the sources of poisoning for our pets, you need to keep all your medications away from your pet to avoid accidental consumption and dispense all the liquids properly.

✓ **Some houseplants are poisonous for your pets.** Dogs like to dig, lick, and taste everything around their place. This may cause serious problems such as irritation or even organ failure. Some of the plants you need to keep an eye on are sago palm, American Yew, Autumn Crocus, and Castor Bean.

✓ **Assign a designated space for them.** You need to tell your pup that s/he has their own place in your house.

This will enable him not just to feel safe and comfortable but also avoiding going to off limits places.

✓ **Keep your poisons away.** Remember to put your detergents, glue, household cleaners, chemicals, and etc. Away from your dog's reach. Mouse and rat poisons are also appetizing to your pet.

✓ **Have a specific boundary.** Puppies are curious in nature. They want to explore every space and see their limits in your own. You need to tell and reprimand them where they belong and where they need to be at all times.

✓ **Don't put them in high spaces.** Puppies are naturally clumsy with fragile bones. Don't tempt them into putting them in great heights that will risk them having an injury or even worse. Don't let kids play with your pet unsupervised unless you want accidents.

✓ **Batteries are not friends.** Any batteries from any devices should be kept out of reach. There are dangerous chemicals stored in the batteries that will cause burns in your Whippet's esophagus.

## Chapter Four: A Sustainable Home for Our Furry Friend

Bringing your first pet home is exciting. However, you should be aware of all the dangers your puppy will have, not only at home, but also outside.

# Chapter Five: Feeding and Nutritional Guide for Your Whippets

We have gone a long way without dearest Whippet. You have decided that you are ready to commit into taking care a dog for around 11 to 15 years. Let us continue knowing the pet that will make your life active and happy. In this portion, we will introduce you feeding and nutrition guide for your pet Whippet.

## Nutrition 101

Just like us, Whippets are omnivores. They will eat any kind of food served to them. However, you should still provide the basic nutrients to promote good health and happy life for your pet.

**Water**

Water is an essential part of life; you should always have a water dish ready for your dog's disposal. You can even give dog food that contains water so your dog could ease up their thirst.

**Proteins**

Meat and plants are needed by your Whippet because it contains nutrients that will keep its body functional and healthy. Animal proteins such as a meat has a high protein value unlike you plant proteins (vegetable)

**Minerals**

Minerals are not a source of energy for dogs. So, why do your dog's need them so much? It aids them into keeping your Whippet's bones and teeth strong, helps in metabolism, and helps in fluid balance in the body.

## Fats

Fats are one way to promote healthy dog fur and skin. Fats also provide that yummy taste which enables your dog to eat more. Also, fats carry vitamins A, D, E, K which is important to the body. However, do not give too much fat.

## Vitamin

You need to supply your Whippet with enough vitamins for her metabolism to function normally. Vitamins are catalysts to help in enzyme reaction. However, you should not give vitamin supplements unless directed by the vet.

## Carbohydrates

Carbohydrates keep your Whippet's intestine healthy that would prevent constipation and diarrhea. Also, it will give energy to their body tissues. You need to set up an appointment with your vet to know what other nutrients your dog needs specifically.

## The Best Dog Food for Your Whippet

In the perfect world, there would only be one kind dog food available However, your pet is presented with many options and making us believe that what they sell is the best in the market. Choosing the best dog food is difficult because they all present the as the healthiest and the most affordable for your dog. We will give you a lot of information about the dog food.

## Characteristics of a Great Dog Food

People will feed their dog's wet or dry food. Although it might not be as appealing as it sounds, it contains all the necessary nutrients that your dog needs to be healthy. High grade commercial food has undergone a lot of testing by specialists.

Your Whippet will also get nutrients from fruits, vegetables, and other grains. These foods are essential source of fiber, minerals, and vitamins. A great dog food will contain the best kind of nutrients suited for the dog's need.

## Myths and Misinformation

There is a wealth of misinformation about dog food and dog nutrition on the Internet. You can sort through it by researching thoroughly. You should check if these things are backed up with scientific evidence. Other than that, these evidences should be supported by a credible source, like a scientific study, veterinarian, or even a nutritionist.

## Reading the Food Label

You can determine the grade of the dog food through its label. If it is a good dog food, all the ingredients are easier to read. There are eight things you need to find in the label:

✓ Product name

✓ Statement of nutritional adequacy

✓ Guaranteed analysis

✓ List of ingredients

✓ Feeding guidelines

✓ Net weight of the product

✓ Name and address of the manufacturer

✓ Intended animal species (i.e. dog or cat)

**What Your Whippet Needs to Avoid**

**Chocolate:** Chocolates are bad for your dog. It has been recently reported that it is used to kill coyotes.

**Brittle Bones:** Cooked bones could choking, pierced intestinal walls, and even intestinal blockage. It is brittle and can cause a choking hazard for your dogs.

**Unattended Human Food:** Your whippet could stealthily eat your human food to teach you a lesson. You should not leave your food out as some food might be in danger for your dog's health.

**Garbage:** Garbage is a treasure for your whippets, although you can also teach the skill no rummage through garbage.

*How Much Should You Feed Your Dog?*

You just follow the manufacturer's guideline to know how much food you should feed your whippet, if you will be feeding it store bought dog food. If your dog is getting fat and loses its curviness, you should lessen the amount.

The only way to know the most appropriate amount of food to feed is through the trial and error method because there are many factors you need to consider such as climate, weight, age, and level of activity.

## Picky Eaters

After reading the labels and checking how much your Whippet should eat, you are ready to feed your dog. Whippets are generally easy - going eaters, but some might not like to eat the food that you have served it. You should be ready and strict with the feeding guidelines of your Whippet. Administer punishment if needed, your pet should follow you, not the other way around.

## When to Feed Your Dog

The best time to feed your dog is after each walk. The exercise will increase food intake and lessen his pickiness as an eater. Also, you should feed your dog at the same time each day; this will make a great routine for your dog. You can divide each meal into two and be given each walk. Start by giving your dog a small amount of food and remove any left overs, if you see a change of appetite, increase the quantity. Don't make food readily available for them; let them know that you are in charge to create a better feeding schedule for them.

# Chapter Six: Grooming 101

Grooming is an essential task for your pet. You will help your Whippet maintain a great look to maintain good health. In this chapter, we will be giving you tips and techniques in grooming your Whippet. You will gain a lot of new knowledge about your dearest pet. The Whippet's silky but short coat is very easy to maintain. Its short coat will definitely keep your house free from loose hair and dirt. Also, this coat is odorless so your house won't stink if your dog has not slept for days. Other than that, there is little to no shedding of its fur. You do not need to cut its fur too much but you need to routinely bathe your dog.

## Grooming Your Whippet

Grooming your whippet is very easy; you just need a weekly brushing using a glove. This will ensure that your dog is free from impurities and dead hair. You should buy an appropriate dog shampoo, because the human and dog have different pH levels thus requiring different products.

Just like any other dogs, Whippets do not really like water. But, you can achieve a great bath time through routine, massage, and cuddling session. You can also give treats after each bath time. To avoid any problems, make sure that you put a rubber mat. Your dog will be very relaxed and comfortable.

## Nail Care

Weekly nail trimming is essential to your dog's grooming session. Long nails could be the cause of your dog's discomfort that will turn to discomfort. To create a good manicure session, always begin when the Whippet is still young. You just cut a small portion of the nail and reward with a treat and praise. It is best to trim the nail slowly than all at once.

Always be careful in cutting your dog's nail, as you do not want to cut too close and too quickly and might cause bleeding. Although you might be alerted and is painful for your dog; this injury is self - healing. Here are several techniques into grooming your dog:

✓ Ears

- Check for signs of inflammation, discharge or foul smell.

- If there is a waxy matter that looks like coffee grounds, it is a sign of infestation. Talk to your vet immediately.

✓ Teeth

- Brush your dog's teeth to prevent tartar build up

- A chew bone might be more effective than brushing.

We have just discussed how to groom your dog. You should allot time and energy in this procedure to keep your dog healthy, it might not be easy at first, but you'll get the hang of it. On the other hand, you might hurt your pet if you groom it incorrectly. There might be bleeding if done improperly. You can ask assistance from a friend or even hire a groomer to know where and how to cut your Whippet's fur and nails.

# Chapter Seven: Whippets as Show Dogs

Some Whippets are bred to be show dogs. If you are headed to this path, there are many things that you need to do to know the breed and show standard for the dog. Winning or being in show is a great deal for both of your pet and the owner. But, you must work hard to learn the breed standard to fully qualify in shows. There are many variations of Whippets that you need to look out for. These faults might not be accepted by shows as they do not comply with the American Kennel Club (AKC) standards.

*Whippet Breed Standard:*

Read on to know more:

✓ **General Appearance**
- ■ Medium size
- ■ Appears to be elegant, fit, denotes great speed, power, balance without being coarse
- ■ Can cover a lot of distance without losing motion
- ■ Must be balanced in power and strength, elegance and grace.
- ■ There is symmetry in outline, muscle development, and gait.

✓ **Size, Proportion, Substance**
- ■ 19 to 22 inches for dogs; 18 to 21 inches for bitches
- ■ Any other variation is disqualified

✓ **Head**
- ■ Appears to be intelligent and alert.
- ■ Has large oval eyes; color must be dark brown to black
- ■ Any other variation is disqualified

✓ **Skull**

- Lean and long
- fairly wide between the ears, scarcely perceptible stop

✓ **Muzzle**

- Powerful and strong
- The look must denote a strong strength of bite
- Your dog might be penalized if there is not under jaw.
- There should be a uniform in pigment in nose leather.
- Teeth should be closely over, creating a scissor bite.
- Teeth should be strong and white.

✓ **Neck, Topline, Body**

- Long, clean, muscular neck
- Its back should be firm, well - muscled, broad.
- The Whippet's backline should run smoothly from withers, creating a graceful natural arch
- There must be a dip behind the blades
- Ribs must be well sprung but does not have a barrel shape.
- No hollow space between forelegs.
- It has a long and tapering tail
- The tail must be in a low gentle upward curve when running or in motion

✓ Forequarters

- Long shoulder blades
- Has flat but well laid back muscles
- Equal upper arm length.
- Straight points of the elbow
- Steep shoulder
- Straight forelegs which gives an appearance of strength and substance.
- Strong, slightly bent, and flexible pasterns
- Any deformities are disqualified
- Well formed, hard, thick pads for both feet.

✓ Hindquarters
- Powerful and long
- Broad and muscular thighs; long and flat muscles; well bent stifles

✓ Coat
- Firm, smooth, close, and short

✓ Gait
- Free moving, low, and smooth
- Strong drive in hindquarters
- Great freedom in action when viewed from its side

- The forelegs come close to the ground with a long, low reach
- Has a strong propelling hind legs


✓ Temperament
  - Amiable
  - capable of great intensity during sporting pursuits
  - Friendly
  - Gentle

## *Tips for Training in a Dog Show:*

✓ You must begin with a Whippet puppy
✓ Find a show dog parents
✓ Find a breeder that will teach you in dog show training, s/he will also teach you the basics.

## Qualification to Compete in Show:
✓ Six months old
✓ No faults according to breed standards
✓ not to be spayed or neutered
✓ if male must have two descended testicles

**Other Qualifications:**

- ✓ be healthy and in good physical condition
- ✓ trot about the ring
- ✓ pose when stopped
- ✓ allow the judge's handling without shyness
- ✓ be able to cope with the noisy and stressful environment of the show.
- ✓ stand on a table

## *Whippet Training 101*

Whippet training will surely make your life easier and more enjoyable. You can start your Whippet training through a basic training program.

The program does not need to be fancy or demanding, take a lot of time and money, but make sure that the program can be done at home. You just need to commit yourself to train your whippet.

Many untrained whippet will be very wild and rowdy, to prevent this fate, you need to engage in several activities that are both rewarding and fun for you and your pet. You will surely be able to enjoy the companionship in the years to come.

Your dog speaks another unknown language but will be receptive to humans that they know our body language and words. This will help you train your Whippet. You should be clear in what you want to teach your pet to create a happy and enjoyable life.

Training your dogs is the bridge to fully understand your dog. Not only is this valuable in shows, you could also benefit from this in your everyday home. Training is difficult but you need to make sure that you give enough rewards to your Whippet for it to aim higher and better.

Fortunately, Whippets are the most obedient among the sight hounds. They respond well to techniques. However, whippets will not please you if they do not want to. You just need to establish basic rules and your authority over the dog. You will have fun teaching him as well as learning from him.

Whippets are whimsical and clever and sometimes would try to outsmart you in so many ways. This is the one of the reasons why living with an intelligent pet is beautiful. Whippet training is not only for the dog, but you, as the trainer, will learn self - control, patience, and observational skills. Be ready for all the surprises the training might have.

Here are just some of the training techniques you need to know:

✓ You don't want to train if you are tired or upset

✓ Your dog will feel that you are upset or not in the mood to train. Remember that our dogs are very receptive to moods. If you are not focused, you will not train your pet easily.

✓ Training should be done before meals

✓ If toys and praises are not doing the trick. You can also give food as reward to get your pet's attention.

✓ Train your dog after it exercises

✓ Take your dog for a walk and have a quick exercise to relax and open your Whippet's mind to training. If the dog is just at home, s/he might not listen to you fully.

✓ Ignore what s/he lacks instead reward everything s/he has done right.

✓ Remember to have a positive attitude. You want your Whippet to know how to succeed but not to be afraid of failing.

✓ The training should be sweet and short

- ✓ Lessen the time. Whippets respond well with short session, i.e. five to ten minutes, rather than long ones.

- ✓ Always be happy every after training session

- ✓ Don't dwell too much on the mistakes of your dog. You can add additional small exercises so your dog will be happy in the end of the session.

- ✓ Always remember to have fun

- ✓ Do not get bored. Finish the training on the correct mood. Leave the session with your pet wanting for more. You will keep your dog's attention much higher for the next session.

Here are some other techniques for you to train your Whippet:

- ✓ Start when the puppy first arrives home. Make sure that you let your Whippet know who is in charge and what s/he need to do.

- ✓ Make sure you housebreak your pet immediately, other than that, you can travel with your pet to know if it will be behaved. If it does not, buy a crate to have a breeze when travelling.

- ✓ House train your pet early. House training can take a number of days. Do not give up and be confident that your dog will learn something from you.

- ✓ Teach your puppies using puppy training games and hey fido!

- ✓ Notice if your dog is aggressive to other dogs. Find out the best way to stop this behaviour towards other dogs.

- ✓ Train your dog using a leash. It may be difficult, but it will be a breeze to train it using a leash.

- ✓ Try on new activities to 'trick' your pet into training.

These are just some things you need to remember when showing your pet. You may need to comply with a lot of things before you actually compete. The competition will be the hardest as you need to pass several skills test to prove your pet's skill.

# Chapter Eight: Breeding Your Whippet

Breeding is a way to continue the lineage of your pet. Some might breed their pet for specific purposes. Should you consider doing this task, there are lot of things you need to remember before you even breed your pet. There are steps that you need to take before you even decide what to do. Here, we will talk about those things to consider before pushing yourself to breed those whippets.

## Should I Breed My Pet?

You should study the lineage of your pet before you decide to breed. Your dog should be fit from genetic health up to its personal health. You need to make sure that your Whippet has an essential contribution to the Whippet society, such as in conformation, agility, racing, or lure racing. Your pups should be able to perform the purpose of hunter and sprinter. If there are faults in your pet, it is better not to breed it to not pass the faults in future generations.

## Why Should I Not Breed My Pet?

There are many things for you to consider why you should not breed your own pet. Keep the following things in mind:

✓ There are still many dogs that need homes in the United States. Many shelters areas still filled with millions of pets that are in fear of being euthanized. You should not add more dogs because you want to breed them.

✓ You should not breed your pet if it comes from a backyard breeder or a pet store. These locations did not care for the history and genetic history of the Whippets.

✓ Do not breed your whippet if it has certain problems such as cancer, deafness, genetic eye defects, overbites, undescended testicles and myostatin mutations. These problems may be passed on to their puppies.

✓ You should also look at the temperament of your dog. If your bitch is too aggressive, it might kill its litter or be overprotective.

**Test Your Whippets:**

Test your whippet dogs for the following medical exams:

✓ The CERF (Canine Eye Registration Foundation) Exam will test for eye disease. The CERF should be done once a year.

✓ The BAER (Brain stem Auditory Evoked Response) Test is a test to determine whether your dog can hear.

✓ Cardiac Clearance Exams is done to check injuries, genetic anomalies, and other ailments that may affect Whippet.

✓ DNA test for the Myostatin gene (double muscle gene).

## The Birthing Process

Dogs can deliver their own puppies without any complications or assistance. But, it is still comforting to know that your pet will deliver the puppy without any complications, hitches, and on schedule.

You might be scared on the birthing process but we will guide you in the birthing process.

## Before the Birthing Process

Dog pregnancy is from 56 to 69 days; large breeds such as Whippets often deliver their puppies late.

Two weeks before the due date, you need to take the temperature at noon. You need an oral or rectal thermometer to do so, the ideal temperature is between 101 to 102.5 Fahrenheit. If your Whippet's temperature falls back to 100 Fahrenheit, you need to deliver the puppies immediately.

## Stage One of Labor

In this stage, the cervix dilates and contractions begin. Just like human contractions, dog contractions are perplexing and even very painful. Your dog will become very restless and uncomfortable. She will pant, shiver, and pace around. Some dogs might not eat and vomit or some may whine loudly. Other dogs may build nests to pass time. Although Uterine Contractions are easily occurring, you might not notice this immediately. This stage lasts for six to eighteen hours.

At the end of this stage, your dog's cervix will be completely dilated so the puppies can pass by easily.

## The Stage Two

In this stage, contractions will be more painful. The placental water sack will break and straw - colored fluid will pass. More placentas will be expelled after each puppy or at periods within the labor. Puppies usually come out every half hour after forceful straining.

When the puppies come out, the mother will clean the puppies through licking, she will as well bite off the umbilical cord. The mother should be the one to do this as this promotes bonding and recognition of love between them. The licking will stimulate breath and circulation for the puppies. If the mother can't do this process, you should be the own to tear the sack and lick the puppies to clear away all the fluids and let the puppy breathe. The mother will want to eat afterwards. Provide enough food and water.

## The Final Stage

This stage happens when all the puppies have been expelled, along with the fluid, placenta, and blood.

The midwifery stage happens after thirty-two days of pregnancy. The mother's appetite will increase; the mother will eat twice as much as she usually does. When she is producing her milk, the food consumption will increase even further. You need to buy great puppy food for her to eat. If you have bought great brand, you should not give any other supplements. You need to provide normal exercise and training to help the mother.

These are some of the things for you to remember when you want to breed your pet. You need to take note of these steps as you will be required to go through with your mother.

# Chapter Nine: Basic Health Hacks for Your Whippets

Taking care of a pet is a big task. You start with its birth; you also need to take care of its health needs. You need to be aware of all the things as they might happen to your pet. You need to know all the possibilities in the future. In this section, we will give you essential information about the common diseases of your pet as well as signs and symptoms.

*Heart Diseases*

There are many heart diseases that might attack your pet. Heart diseases are common to dogs and specialists will screen for possibilities of heart problems. There are many ways for you to know if your dog has heart problem, you may need to contact a veterinary for proper treatment and detection. Some of the heart diseases are the following:

## Mitral Valve Insufficiency

- Common to older dogs

- The mitral valve in the left atrium and left ventricle starts to fail. This valve prevents backflow of blood within the heart.

- Blood pressure is the highest in the left ventricle, when it fails, it might cause problems such as high blood pressure.

**Symptoms:**

- Coughing, especially after  excitement, exercise, or when the animal has first got up after sleeping
- Signs of tiredness and weakness

**Treatment:**

- Medications that strengthen and coordinate the muscles' contractions
- Diuretics that will remove the excess fluid
- Low sodium diet.

## Immune Mediated Disease

- It is the destruction of the body's own cell by the immune system.
- Autoimmune disease is result of the malfunction of immune system; it happens when the self - treats itself as foreign and will destroy it.
- If left untreated, it could result to death.

**Cause:**

- Tends to run in the family

**Treatment:**

- Early treatment is important for this disease because it may become life threatening very quickly.

## Steroid Responsive Meningitis

- This is caused by the immune system targeting the lining of the spinal cord or brain.
- Affects younger dogs
- Does not respond well with anti-inflammatories or antibiotics

### Treatment:

- Prednisolone (steroids) at an initial high immunosuppressive dose. You should limit the intake of steroids as your dog might get addicted to it easily.
- Zantac could also be given during gastro-protectant

## Systemic Lupus Erythematosus

- Fatal and rare chronic disease.
- This targets several organs such as kidney, blood, nervous system, skin, joints.

### Symptoms:

- Polyarthritis (lameness in several joints)
- shifting lameness
- skin sores

- blood  disorders
- fevers

**Treatment:**

- Steroids
- A second immune- suppressing drug such as Azathioprine will be necessary

**Symptoms include the following:**

## Immune Mediated Haemolytic Anaemia

Your dog will become very lethargy because it lacks oxygen in the blood. Your dog may even collapse due to lack of oxygen.

**Symptoms:**

- Positive Coombs test
- jaundice which causes yellow pale eyes
- Enlargement of the spleen
- Enlargement of lymph nodes
- Scabby or crusty extremities
- Anaemia can be seen through very pale gums.
- Free haemoglobin that is seen in blood and urine
- exhaustion and lethargy

## Thrombocytopenia

This is a condition where the platelet count is lower than normal. There are several causes such as cancer, some infections and even some medications.

**Symptoms:**

- Lethargy
- Bleeding gums
- Nosebleeds
- Prolonged bleeding after injury
- Loss of appetite
- Weakness
- Pale membranes which can be seen in pale eyes and gums
- Unexplained bruising, especially on the belly
- Black tarry stools or bloody stools
- Blood in the urine
- Bleeding eyes

**Treatment:**

- A course of steroids that suppresses the immune system through stopping the destruction of platelets.
- Drug therapy

## Addison's Disease (Canine Hyoadrenocorticism)

- This is due to the auto-antibody production against the adrenal glands.

- The immune system targets and destroys the adrenal glands.

- The result of this disease is the deficiency of two hormones glucocorticoids and mineralocorticoids. Cortisol fights stress and maintains blood sugar while aldosterone that regulates, water, potassium, and chloride in the body.

- Addison's can still be treatable and your dog will be stable and have an enjoyable and normal life.

- If you withdraw the steroid too quickly, it can result to other Addison's symptoms.

- This disease can be progressive or can present itself as a crisis, either way, it should be treated immediately.

The symptomss include:
- Sickness
- Dehydration
- Muscle weakness

- lethargy
- Lack of appetite
- Excess drinking
- Diarrhea that may contain blood
- Abdominal pain
- Increased urine production
- Weight loss
- cold to the touch, shaky,
- Depression
- Sudden collapse and shock
- Kidney failure

Your vet needs to perform various tests to confirm the disease; one test is the ACTH simulation test.

The treatment involves:

- Great dedication and observation of the owner. This is done to stabilize the condition; vet visits will help monitor the response to treatment.

- You can also consider steroid replacement therapy. Also, you need to have daily salt replacement such as Florinef

- All the medications should be fitted to the dog and needs to be closely monitored until the dog become stable.

- You also need to mention if the dog gets stressed when it has an Addison disease. Stress is an important factor; a stressed dog may need to have his/her medication changed to be better. Your dog needs to avoid mental and physical stress if possible.

- You should follow and administer the medication exactly, any alterations or changes must not be done. Also, if there is vomiting, you need to report it immediately to your vet.

- You should do regular visits to your vet until it is stable.

## Hypothyroidism

- This is the disorder of the thyroid gland.

- Thyroixine which regulates metabolism of almost all the body's system is the one being attacked by the hypothyroidism.

- Many normal functions would be affected greatly if there is not enough thyroxine.

- The destruction of the gland by the body's own immune system is the most common cause of this disease.

- The destruction of the thyroid begins very early in a dog's life. However, the symptoms take years to be evident and the gland to be completely destroyed.

- You can use the period to fully assess the severity of the dog's case.

- You can easily manage hypothyroidism if you have diagnosed it early. Hypothyroidism can't be cured but can be managed.

- The most difficult part is the diagnosis, because the symptoms dictate different conditions. You may need your vet for proper assessment.

**Signs of Hypothyroidism;**

✓ Hair loss

✓ Thinning of the skin

✓ Black pigmentation of the skin

✓ Scurf (dandruff)

✓ Lethargy

✓ Anxiety

✓ Unexplained aggression

✓ Hyperactivity

✓ Seizures

✓ Obesity

✓ Seeks warm places to hide and lie down due to cold intolerance

✓ Reproductive problems.

✓ Lipidosis or the depositing of fat in the cornea of the eye

✓ Dry eye (keratitis sicca)

✓ Constipation

✓ Slow heart rate (bradycardia)

✓ Muscle weakness

✓ Diarrhea

✓ Vomiting

Your vet will perform the test called baseline T4 Level. This is the usual test to know if your dog has hypothyroidism. If the result returns 'in range', your vet will consider that the dog does not have hypothyroidism. However, this is not the most definite test.

The best way to assess thyroid function is through conducting a full thyroid panel that measures T4, Free T4, and TSH (Thyroid stimulating hormone). Sighthounds have a lower baseline T4 than any other dogs. Other than that, old dogs have lower T4, you, as well as your vet, should be reminded of this.

**Treatment for Hypothyroidism:**

- Daily doses of Thyroxin, which continues for life. You need to monitor the dog closely and you should follow all the prescribed doses.

- Overdose will cause restlessness, weight loss, anxiety, excessive drinking and hyperactivity.

- You need to have constant vet consultation to treat this.

Your dog will improve quickly. It will become energetic, skin will be livelier. This will happen after the treatment begins.

## Symmetrical Lupoid Onychoclystrophy

- This disease targets the nail beds.

- Your dog's nail will break and fall out. If they regrow, it will break and fall out again.

- Some might diagnose this as a fungal infection, but will not treat this fully.

- This disease is thought to be an autoimmune disease. The immune system targets the nail as a foreign substance and wants to destroy it.

- There is research on going for this rare form of disease.

**Signs and symptoms:**

✓ Nail loss, often multiple

✓ Licking and chewing of nails

✓ Nails grow back deformed, crusty and fall off again

✓ possible severe bleeding when nails come off

✓ infection and smell

✓ Separation of nails from the quick inside

✓ pain and limping

✓ oozing around the nail bed

**Diagnosis:**

✓ You should rule out fungal infections

✓ Antibiotics will not help to cure this disease.

✓ Correct diagnosis will include the amputation of the end part of the toe for biopsy.

The treatment for this disease is only trial and error. Each dog will have different treatment fitted for them. Loose nails that cause much pain need to be removed.

The first treatment for this is essential fatty acids along with vitamin E, tetracycline and niacinamide. Also, your vet could advice you steroid treatment can also be used if the treatments won't work.

You should give pain medication to your dog especially if the pain is severe. Your vet will give you the best treatment for your dog. This disease will remain forever but becomes manageable. Your dog's nail will fall off and regrow, but will fall off again if it becomes long enough.

**Immune Mediated Polyarthritis**

- Joint disease wherein the immune system attacks the articular surface of the joints, which creates an inflammatory response.

- The two types of this disease is erosive and the non-erosive.

- The most common form is the non-erosive which is associated with Systemic Lupus

- This disease can also be associated with intestinal disease, cancer, or serious infection.

The symptoms for this disease include:

- Reluctance to move
- Stiffness
- Swelling of the joints can be present
- Lethargy
- High temperature
- Lack of appetite
- Lameness which could shift among the legs
- Pain on opening mouth
- Painful swollen joints that most of the time affects the same joints in the right and left limbs.
- In some cases, there will be dislocation of joints due to local ligament rupture. Also, there is an excessive range of movement.
- Cracking, clicking, or grating sensation also called the Crepitus is also present when the joints are also used.

You can know how severe the disease if there is stiffness or a complete inability to walk or stand. You should contact your vet if your suspect that your dog has immune mediated polyarthritis. There are many tests that your vet will do to determine the type of polyarthritis and its causes.

The treatment will heavily depend on the cause. Spontaneous recovery can happen with vaccine reactions, in other cases high doses of steroids will be prescribed.

Recovery time is usually rapid but the dog may relapse, this will result to lifetime steroid medication. Other immunosuppressing drugs may be used f the dosage needed is too high to control the disease.

This disease is difficult both to diagnose and treat. Sometimes, it may require having your dog to be in lifelong steroid treatment, and the side effects of the steroid should also be managed. You need to give the lowest dosage that will control the symptoms in order to maintain the quality of life. You may need to contact a vet specialist to treat your Whippet.

There are several symptoms of polyarthritis, such as:

- Dermatitis
- Glomerulonephritis (kidney disease)
- Meningitis
- Myositis
- Thrombocytopenia
- Anemia

## Cushings Disease (Hyperadrenocorticism)

- This condition is common in older dogs.

- A symptom may mimic the aging process which is difficult to differentiate.

- Fortunately, this condition is easily treatable that will enable your dog to have a better lifestyle especially when medicated.

- This condition is caused by a tumour in adrenal glands located near the kidneys or in the pituitary gland which is located near the brain.

- Another cause of the Cushings could be treatment of other diseases using corticosteroids which triggers the symptom of the disease.

- The result of this disease, primarily, is pituitary tumour. This tumor is usually slow and small growing but sends continuous signals to Adrenal glands to continually produce corticol hormones. Normally, the dog's body will stop producing corticol hormones when it reaches the correct level. However, in a dog with Cushings disease, the pituitary gland will continue produce adrenal gland to produce more hormone.

- Adrenal gland tumor is less common but still has the same results - the nonstop production of corticol hormones.

There are many symptoms and vary from dogs, they will progress very slowly.

The most common symptoms include:

- excessive drinking
- increased urination
- Previously house trained dogs may begin to have "accidents"
- increased appetite
- food stealing
- excessive hunger
- pot-bellied look
- excess panting
- thinning hair or baldness
- thin, wrinkled or dark coloured skin
- Susceptibility to infections, especially urinary or skin infections
- weight gain
- loss of muscle
- bony, skull-like look to the head
- bruised skin, slow healing of cuts
- tiredness, reluctance to walk
- Diabetes
- pancreatitis
- seizures

Arthritic dog or dogs with allergies seems to improve due to the corticosteroid the dogs' body is producing. If you can see that your dog is drinking a lot more, increase in appetite, and even thinning of coat, you can deduce that Cushings is the problem.

You need to visit your vet because they are some tests that could diagnose this disease. There are a lot of drugs that can be used to fight Cushings. These options will be discussed by your vet.

If you do not treat Cushings, it may progress and your dog will contract many infections, some may even develop hypothyroidism, heart failure, blood clots, pancreatitis, liver and kidney failure.

This disease can be easily managed and your dog's quality of life will improve tremendously. It willl require great commitment from the owner to keep the dog stable and have a great life quality.

## Megaesophagus

✓ This condition will affect the esophagus, the tube that transports food from the mouth up to the stomach. In normal dogs, the esophagus relaxes and constricts that forces food into the stomach which is called the peristalsis.

✓ In affected dogs, the esophagus will lose its ability to remain flaccid and contract. They are unable to push the ingested food into the stomach, or it simply sits there until it has regurgitated.

✓ There could also be cases of aspiration pneumonia wherein the reflex that prevents breathing at the same food is swallowed is also lost. Affected dogs might inhale the food instead of ingesting it.

✓ Some signs of aspiration pneumonia are general lethargy and coughing.

✓ You need to keep a close eye to your dog especially what it intakes, eats, or even drinks anything. Your dog needs to sit for at least 10 minutes after or be held in sitting or begging position.

✓ You can administer food at regular intervals (some even two to three hours) but in smaller quantities.

✓ You need to make sure that the dog has sufficient water and caloric intake.

✓ You can pursue a raw diet for whippets with this condition.

✓ You may want to have a feeding chair to keep your dog in an upward position and to aid the passage of its food up to its stomach.

✓ You need to see the difference of regurgitation in megaesophagus and vomiting.

**FORMS OF THE DISEASE**

CONGENITAL

a) This is present at birth or afterwards. is present at birth or soon afterwards

b) Puppies born with this disease have poor nerve development but could improve when it grows up.

c) There is a band of tissue, normally dissolved before birth. This constricts esophagus that could cause regurgitation. This could be surgically removed and the chances of the survival are high.

ACQUIRED

d) This usually appears in older dogs.

e) These have several treatments and may require veterinary diagnosis.

Unfortunately, the condition cannot be cured but can be easily managed. The treatment involves experimentation with feeding and food consistency. You need to be dedicated and vigilant to improve the life of your dog. Some drugs may assist with gastric movement.

Symptoms include the following:

- Weight loss
- Discharge from nose
- Regurgitation of food and water
- High temperature
- Cough
- Difficulty breathing
- Salivation

- Smelly breath

## Causes of Aquired Megaesophagus

- Myasthenia Gravis is an auto-immune condition wherein the muscle or nerve junctions are destroyed therefore affecting the peristalsis.

- Narrowing due to trauma or obstruction

## Corns

✓ Corns are hard area on each pad which only occur in whippets and Greyhound. People do not know why corns are common between these breeds. Some people suggest that there is a lack of fatty tissues in each pad, while some say this is because of a virus.

✓ It is known that corn development runs in the family and should not be taken lightly.

✓ These are very painful for the dog and can seriously affect the quality of life.

✓ They may be developed in dogs under a year old and affect their entire life. However some dogs may only develop it in the later parts of their life.

**Signs and symptoms:**

- Dog pulls over to the ground when walking
- Lameness
- Being lame on hard surfaces but fine on carpet and soft grass
- There are tiny black dot which is usually round or raised on skin on the pads.

Unfortunately, vets can't easily diagnose this disease as they have never seen one. However, you can tell if the dog has corns if the dogs react even to the slightest pressure will be very painful for them. You should treat corns immediately, as they will become bigger, more painful, and harder if left untreated.

There are a lot of ways to treat corns but no definite cure for it. You should have a discussion with your vet on how to keep your dog free from any pain, as this is the only option that you will have:

✓ **Hulling.** One of the treatments you can have. This process removes corn through leverage but it can and must be only done by your vet. However, the corn will return, but it can still be removed again.

✓ **Surgery.** This process will remove all the corn up to its root under anaesthetic. You may want to consult an experienced vet to remove the corn. However, the corn may still return.

✓ Do not use human corn softening treatments as they will not really work.

✓ In some cases, amputation may be the only option. However, this increases pressure on remaining toes, that may cause corn on the other toe.

You should not make your dog walk on hard surfaces if it suffers from corn. You should carpet your hard floors at home and only have exercises on soft places. There are padded boots available that help reduces the pain that they will feel if your dog still needs to walk on hard surfaces.

# Cheat Sheet for Whippet Dogs

You have read and gathered a lot of information about Whippets, it is now time to get your own dog and apply these theories into real life.

You need to look up additional information in other books or websites for further knowledge. This will help you gain a lot of information about the breed, where to find the best breeder, and maintain a happy and healthy puppy or adult dog. In this part, we will summarize all the things we have discussed in the previous sections. You need to know these things if you still want to pursue having whippets as your pet.

## Whippet's Basic Information

**Origin:** England

**Pedigree:** crossbreed of Greyhound and many possible terriers

**Breed Size:** big size

**Body Type and Appearance:** Has a classic 'inverted s' line. It has a deep chest and trim waist. It has a lean head connected to a long, arched neck. They possess sturdy and slim legs that is combined with agile, fleet-footed athlete.

**Group:** Hound Group

**Height:** 19 - 22 in (Male), 18 - 21 in (Female)

**Weight:** 18 - 48 pounds. Males average 34 pounds and 29 pounds for female

**Coat Length:** short, close

**Coat Texture:** smooth and firm

**Color:** brindle, white, black, fawn, blue, red

**Temperament:** curious, playful, willing to approach people, affectionate, lively, gentle, intelligent, quiet, friendly

**Strangers:** friendly around strangers

**Other Dogs**: gets along well with other dogs

**Other Pets**: may get along well with other pets if properly socialized, may chase small pets

**Training**: loves to be trained by their humans

**Exercise Needs**: needs daily exercise through running or walking around a fenced yard

**Health Conditions**: generally healthy but may be affected by the following illnesses: anesthesia sensitivity, deafness, eye diseases, von willebrand's disease

**Lifespan**: average 12 to 15 years

*Home Requirements*

**Recommended Accessories**: toys, collar, harness, grooming supplies crate, dog bed, food/water dishes, leash,

**Collar and Harness**: sized by weight

**Grooming Supplies**: comb, nail clipper, glove for the owners protection

**Grooming Frequency**: once a month, to remove dead hair and dead skin cells

**Energy Level**: alert and playful outside, lazy and slouch when inside the house

**Exercise Requirements**:  exercise is needed to shed off excess energy

**Crate**:  recommended for transport

**Crate Size**:  large

**Food/Water**:  preferably stainless steel or ceramic bowls

**Toys**: do not give too much toys as it may create a playful environment at home.

**Training**: responds well to obedience training

*Nutritional Needs*

**Nutritional Needs**: fats, vitamins, minerals, water, protein, carbohydrate

**Calorie Needs**: a lot of calories are needed due to its large size and activity

**Amount to Feed (puppy):** consult your vet, try the trial and error method

**Amount to Feed (adult)**: you can start with the suggested size portion in the package

**Important Ingredients**: fresh animal protein (chicken, beef, lamb, turkey, eggs), digestible carbohydrates (rice, oats, barley), animal fats

**Important Minerals**: calcium, magnesium, iron, copper and manganese phosphorus, potassium

**Important Vitamins**: , Vitamin B-12, Vitamin D, Vitamin A, Vitamin C

**Certifications**: AAFCO statement of nutritional adequacy; protein at top of ingredients list; no artificial flavors, dyes, preservatives

## Breeding Information

**Age of First Heat**: around 6 or 7 months (or earlier)

**Heat (Estrus) Cycle**: 15 to 21 days

**Frequency**: once or twice a year

**Greatest Fertility**: 11 to 15 days into the cycle

**Gestation Period**: 59 to 63 days

**Pregnancy Detection**: possible after 24 to 25 days, best to wait 45 days for the ultrasound

**Feeding Pregnant Dogs**: maintain normal diet until week 5 or 6 then slightly increase rations

**Signs of Labor**: body temperature drops below normal 100° to 102°F (37.7° to 38.8°C), may be as low as 98°F (36.6°C); dog begins nesting in a dark, quiet place

**Contractions**: period of 10 minutes in waves of 2 to 3 followed by a period of rest

**Whelping**: puppies are born in 1/2 hour increments following 10 to 30 minutes of forceful straining

**Puppies**: born with eyes and ears closed; eyes open at 3 weeks, teeth develop at 10 weeks

**Litter Size**: average 6 to 12 puppies

**Size at Birth**: about 100 pounds or more

**Weaning**: start offering puppy food soaked in water at 6 weeks; fully weaned by 8 weeks

**Socialization**: start as early as possible to prevent puppies from being nervous as an adult

## Glossary of Dog Terms

**Abundism** – Referring to a pup that has markings more prolific than is normal.

**Acariasis** – A type of mite infection.

**ACF** – Australian Pup Federation

**Affix** – A puptery name that follows the pup's registered name; puptery owner, not the breeder of the pup.

**Agouti** – A type of natural coloring pattern in which individual hairs have bands of light and dark coloring.

**Ailurophile** – A person who loves pups.

**Albino** – A type of genetic mutation which results in little to no pigmentation, in the eyes, skin, and coat.

**Allbreed** – Referring to a show that accepts all breeds or a judge who is qualified to judge all breeds.

**Alley Pup** – A non-pedigreed pup.

**Alter** – A desexed pup; a male pup that has been neutered or a female that has been spayed.

**Amino Acid** – The building blocks of protein; there are 22 types for pups, 11 of which can be synthesized and 11 which must come from the diet (see essential amino acid).

**Anestrus** – The period between estrus cycles in a female pup.

**Any Other Variety (AOV)** – A registered pup that doesn't conform to the breed standard.

**ASH** – American Shorthair, a breed of pup.

**Back Cross** – A type of breeding in which the offspring is mated back to the parent.

**Balance** – Referring to the pup's structure; proportional in accordance with the breed standard.

**Barring** – Describing the tabby's striped markings.

**Base Color** – The color of the coat.

**Bicolor** – A pup with patched color and white.

**Blaze** – A white coloring on the face, usually in the shape of an inverted V.

**Bloodline** – The pedigree of the pup.

**Brindle** – A type of coloring, a brownish or tawny coat with streaks of another color.

**Castration** – The surgical removal of a male pup's testicles.

**Pup Show** – An event where pups are shown and judged.

**Puptery** – A registered pup breeder; also, a place where pups may be boarded.

**CFA** – The Pup Fanciers Association.

**Cobby** – A compact body type.

**Colony** – A group of pups living wild outside.

**Color Point** – A type of coat pattern that is controlled by color point alleles; pigmentation on the tail, legs, face, and ears with an ivory or white coat.

**Colostrum** – The first milk produced by a lactating female; contains vital nutrients and antibodies.

**Conformation** – The degree to which a pedigreed pup adheres to the breed standard.

**Cross Breed** – The offspring produced by mating two distinct breeds.

**Dam** – The female parent.

**Declawing** – The surgical removal of the pup's claw and first toe joint.

**Developed Breed** – A breed that was developed through selective breeding and crossing with established breeds.

**Down Hairs** – The short, fine hairs closest to the body which keep the pup warm.

**DSH** – Domestic Shorthair.

**Estrus** – The reproductive cycle in female pups during which she becomes fertile and receptive to mating.

**Fading Pup Syndrome** – Pups that die within the first two weeks after birth; the cause is generally unknown.

**Feral** – A wild, untamed pup of domestic descent.

**Gestation** – Pregnancy; the period during which the fetuses develop in the female's uterus.

**Guard Hairs** – Coarse, outer hairs on the coat.

**Harlequin** – A type of coloring in which there are van markings of any color with the addition of small patches of the same color on the legs and body.

**Inbreeding** – The breeding of related pups within a closed group or breed.

**Kibble** – Another name for dry pup food.

**Lilac** – A type of coat color that is pale pinkish-gray.

**Line** – The pedigree of ancestors; family tree.

**Litter** – The name given to a group of pups born at the same time from a single female.

**Mask** – A type of coloring seen on the face in some breeds.

**Matts** – Knots or tangles in the pup's fur.

**Mittens** – White markings on the feet of a pup.

**Moggie** – Another name for a mixed breed pup.

**Mutation** – A change in the DNA of a cell.

**Muzzle** – The nose and jaws of an animal.

**Natural Breed** – A breed that developed without selective breeding or the assistance of humans.

**Neutering** – Desexing a male pup.

**Open Show** – A show in which spectators are allowed to view the judging.

**Pads** – The thick skin on the bottom of the feet.

**Particolor** – A type of coloration in which there are markings of two or more distinct colors.

**Patched** – A type of coloration in which there is any solid color, tabby, or tortoiseshell color plus white.

**Pedigree** – A purebred pup; the pup's papers showing its family history.

**Pet Quality** – A pup that is not deemed of high enough standard to be shown or bred.

**Piebald** – A pup with white patches of fur.

**Points** – Also color points; markings of contrasting color on the face, ears, legs, and tail.

**Pricked** – Referring to ears that sit upright.

**Purebred** – A pedigreed pup.

**Queen** – An intact female pup.

**Roman Nose** – A type of nose shape with a bump or arch.

**Scruff** – The loose skin on the back of a pup's neck.

**Selective Breeding** – A method of modifying or improving a breed by choosing pups with desirable traits.

**Senior** – A pup that is more than 5 but less than 7 years old.

**Sire** – The male parent of a pup.

**Solid** – Also self; a pup with a single coat color.

**Spay** – Desexing a female pup.

**Stud** – An intact male pup.

**Tabby** – A type of coat pattern consisting of a contrasting color over a ground color.

**Tom Pup** – An intact male pup.

**Tortoiseshell** – A type of coat pattern consisting of a mosaic of red or cream and another base color.

**Tri-Color** – A type of coat pattern consisting of three distinct colors in the coat.

**Tuxedo** – A black and white pup.

**Unaltered** – A pup that has not been desexed.

# Index

# Photo Credits

Page 58 Photo by user ArtbyCharlotte via Pixabay.com,

https://pixabay.com/en/whippet-dog-pet-animal-domestic-2846688/

Page 62 Photo by user 12019 via Pixabay.com,

https://pixabay.com/en/whippet-dachshund-dogs-canines-85583/

Page 72 Photo by user Mabuya via Pixabay.com,

https://pixabay.com/en/nature-animal-dog-whippet-trust-1153766/

Page 79 Photo by user Art By Charlotte via Pixabay.com,

https://pixabay.com/en/whippet-dog-pet-animal-domestic-2855874/

Page 104 Photo by user Mabuya via Pixabay.com,

https://pixabay.com/en/nature-animals-dogs-house-pet-1172215/

# References

**Whippet** – Vetstreet.com

http://www.vetstreet.com/dogs/whippet

**Whippet** – PetMd.com

https://www.petmd.com/dog/breeds/c_dg_whippet#

**The Origin of the Whippet** – Whippet History

https://whippethistory.wordpress.com/2011/02/12/originwhippet/

**Whippet** – Dogtime.com

http://dogtime.com/dog-breeds/whippet#/slide/7

**Whippet: What's Good About 'Em, What's Bad About 'Em** – YourPureBredPuppy.com

http://www.yourpurebredpuppy.com/reviews/whippets.html

**Choosing the Right Bed for Your Dog** – 1800PetMeds.com

https://www.1800petmeds.com/education/choosing-right-dog-bed-23.htm

**Whippet** – American Kennel Club

http://www.akc.org/dog-breeds/whippet/

**How to Groom a Whippet, Dog Skin Problems and Nail Trimming** - TheWhippet.net

https://www.thewhippet.net/groom-a-whippet.html

**Twelve Points to Identifying a Quality Breeder** - AwareWisconsin.com

http://www.awarewisconsin.com/twelve-points-to-identifying-a-quality-breeder/

**10 Point Checklist for Puppy Proofing Your Home** - PreventiveVet.com

https://www.preventivevet.com/dogs/checklist-for-puppy-proofing-your-home

**20 Tips to Puppy Proof Your Home** - Vetwest.com.au

https://www.vetwest.com.au/pet-library/20-tips-to-puppy-proof-your-home

**Understanding your dog's nutritional needs** - Cesarsway.com

https://www.cesarsway.com/dog-care/food-and-treats/understanding-your-dogs-nutritional-needs

**Best Dog Food: Choosing What's Right For Your Dog** – American Kennel Club

https://www.akc.org/expert-advice/nutrition/general-nutrition/best-dog-food-choosing-whats-right-for-your-dog/

**Feeding a Whippet 101**- TheWhippet.net

https://www.thewhippet.net/feeding-a-whippet.html

**Whippet - Breed and Grooming Tips** – Espree.com

https://www.espree.com/breedProfiler/Hound-Group-Whippet-Grooming-Bathing-and-Care/6/96

**Training a Show Dog** - TheWhippet.net

https://www.thewhippet.net/training-a-show-dog.html

**Whippet Training** - TheWhippet.net

https://www.thewhippet.net/whippet-training.html

**Good Breeding** – UtahWhippet.com

http://www.utahwhippet.com/pages/breeding.html

**Canine Labor Stages** - 2ndchance.info

https://www.2ndchance.info/caninelaborstages.htm

http://whippet-health.co.uk/

Feeding Baby
Cynthia Cherry
978-1941070000

Axolotl
Lolly Brown
978-0989658430

Dysautonomia, POTS
Syndrome
Frederick Earlstein
978-0989658485

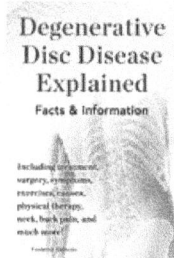

Degenerative Disc
Disease Explained
Frederick Earlstein
978-0989658485

Sinusitis, Hay Fever,
Allergic Rhinitis Explained
Frederick Earlstein
978-1941070024

Wicca
Riley Star
978-1941070130

Zombie Apocalypse
Rex Cutty
978-1941070154

Capybara
Lolly Brown
978-1941070062

Eels As Pets
Lolly Brown
978-1941070167

Scabies and Lice Explained
Frederick Earlstein
978-1941070017

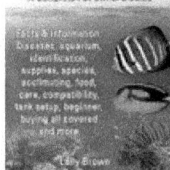

Saltwater Fish As Pets
Lolly Brown
978-0989658461

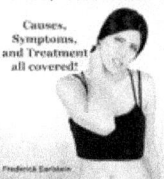

Torticollis Explained
Frederick Earlstein
978-1941070055

Kennel Cough
Lolly Brown
978-0989658409

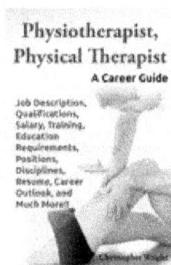

Physiotherapist, Physical
Therapist
Christopher Wright
978-0989658492

Rats, Mice, and Dormice
As Pets
Lolly Brown
978-1941070079

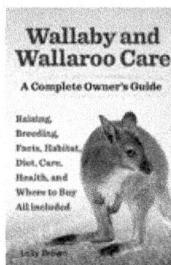

Wallaby and Wallaroo Care
Lolly Brown
978-1941070031

Bodybuilding Supplements
Explained
Jon Shelton
978-1941070239

Demonology
Riley Star
978-19401070314

Pigeon Racing
Lolly Brown
978-1941070307

Dwarf Hamster
Lolly Brown
978-1941070390

Cryptozoology
Rex Cutty
978-1941070406

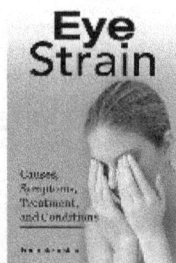

Eye Strain
Frederick Earlstein
978-1941070369

Inez The Miniature Elephant
Asher Ray
978-1941070353

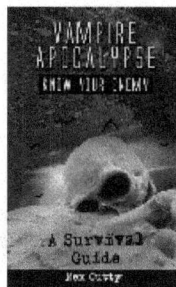

Vampire Apocalypse
Rex Cutty
978-1941070321

www.ingramcontent.com/pod-product-compliance
Lightning Source LLC
Chambersburg PA
CBHW052110090426
42741CB00009B/1748